Trompe L'Oeil
Panels and Panoramas

TROMPE L'OEIL PANELS AND PANORAMAS

DECORATIVE IMAGES

FOR ARTISTS & ARCHITECTS

YANNICK GUÉGAN

W. W. NORTON & COMPANY

New York • London

ALSO BY YANNICK GUÉGAN

The Handbook of Painted Decoration:
The Tools, Materials and Step-by-Step Techniques of Trompe L'Oeil Painting
with Roger Le Puil

Manufacturing by Colorprint Offset
Book design by Gilda Hannah
Production manager: Leeann Graham

Library of Congress Cataloging-in-Publication Data

Guégan, Yannick, 1947–
Trompe l'oeil panels and panoramas: decorative images
for artists & architects/Yannick Guégan
p. cm.
Includes index

ISBN 0-393-73090-5
Decoration and ornament–Trompe l'oeil. 2. Decoration and ornament–
History–20th century. I. Title.

NK 1590.T76 G84 2003
751.7'3—dc21   2002033751

W. W. Norton & Company, Inc.
500 Fifth Avenue, New York, N.Y. 10110
www.wwnorton.com

W. W. Norton & Company Ltd.
Castle House, 75/76 Wells St., London W1T 3QT

1 2 3 4 5 6 7 8 9 0

Contents

❧

PREFACE

✿

". . . that your eyes take in everything and your hands create in total freedom."

My wish, perhaps my calling, is to teach decorative painting and the art of trompe l'oeil around the world. This book is an important step along my own artistic and pedagogical road. Having taught and published on the subject for over thirty years, I now offer a book of designs and studies meant to inspire readers to paint decorations and murals of their own, choosing colors, textures, and subject matter from their own imaginations.

The images in this book are the result of an exciting experiment with students from many of my classes. It is a true collaboration with my often passion ate and always attentive students and colleagues from around the world, who come to the Guégan Institute in Quimiac every year to learn, and also to impart their own knowledge to us all.

A team of artist-decorators and former students helped me to produce this book, contributing to its spirit and work, and fashioning their artwork by apply-

Pages 6-9: **Students at the Guégan Institute working on the Venice panorama (see pages 112-113).**

ing the very techniques I propose in this book. We exchanged ideas and held discussions from which emerged, for example, the belief that the less text included in the book the better. In this way, the images speak for themselves.

This book, however, is not written uniquely for practicing painters and decorators: it is for all those interested in decoration in general. Whether in a personal capacity for amateurs and curious minds, or in a professional capacity for architects, interior decorators, and artists, these images provide inspiration.

I invite readers to embark on a voyage—a convergence of ideas, images, personalities, places, and dreams. From my creations, I invite you to generate your very own.

YANNICK GUÉGAN

INTRODUCTION

❧

This is a book of images. I hope they will become your images. The idea is to inspire, to give you the freedom to create, using elements from the studies and paintings in this book. I invite you to copy with abandon! It is my hope that these images will trigger other ideas and achievements of your own. Follow the examples of the top graduates of the Guégan Institute, whose work you will find in the following pages. As they have been inspired by my own work, you too will discover their works useful in your own projects.

Some of the projects are presented in different stages, ranging from a simple outline to a completed panorama. The act of creation, no matter what its nature, involves a number of steps; yet all creations need not result in a finalized décor. Rather, consider each image in this book as an independent proposal that can be incorporated into one or many images. Thus, all associations of images are possible.

I give little information about trompe l'oeil painting here: I covered these topics in my previous book, *The Handbook of Painted Decoration*. The Technical Notes that follow provide general indications. In this book, I invite you to participate in a dream, a poetic and visual stroll, in which the images are indispensable to its creation.

The images in the book have been loosely grouped thematically, but given the varied subject matter of the paintings, these categories are arbitrary: they offer some organization and useful comparisons, but the images might equally well be arranged in other ways.

You will find at the back of the book a CD-ROM that contains all the trompe l'oeil works reproduced in the book. These screen-resolution TIFF files, usable on Mac or PC, are provided for your convenience in studying the paintings and in transferring the designs for use in your own work.

I hope you will use elements of the models, drawings, and finished paintings in this book to create beautiful decorative paintings somewhere in the world. And for this opportunity, I thank you.

ACKNOWLEDGMENTS

I wish to acknowledge the following students who have contributed to this book:

Monique Elizabé: pages 20-21, 164-65, 171-73, 210-11

Sophie Hustin: pages 22-23, 182-84

Catherine Leclerc: pages 48-49, and participation in the work on pages 52-53

Sylvie Roger: pages 62-63, 98-99

Gisèle Cwern: pages 74-75

Krista Yasvin: pages 160-63

Technical Notes

TERMS

A panorama is generally a large work depicting interior or countryside scenes with definite foreground and background planes. A decorative panel may also be considered a panorama if its size and subject matter are similar. The boundary between decorative panels and panoramas is not strict.

MEDIUMS

Two principal mediums for creating trompe l'oeil art are suggested: acrylic ink and oil.

    Acrylic ink dries quickly, allowing for easy superimpositions; its colors remain bright; it maintains its integrity in light, and it can be diluted with water.

    Oil is the traditional medium. Its slow drying time results in interesting color and texture gradations, and is ideal for superimpositions on acrylic ink. It dilutes with a colored varnish composed of:

- $\frac{1}{3}$ oil
- $\frac{2}{3}$ turpentine
- $\frac{5}{100}$ dryer

COLORS

All work in this book is done using products from Golden Artists Colors, Inc. For a list of their retail stores, visit www.goldenpaints.com. The following is a list of some colors used in the images:

Acrylic ink
    yellow oxide
    red oxide
    raw umber
    raw sienna
    burnt sienna
    green
    ultramarine blue
    titanium white
    carbon black
    diarylide yellow
    naphthol red light
    phthalic blue

Oil

titanium white
Naples yellow
Mars black
French red vermilion
yellow ocher
cobalt blue
raw umber
red ocher
ultramarine deep
chrome yellow medium
permanent Vandyck brown
Prussian blue
raw sienna
burnt sienna
chrome green deep
ivory black

VARNISH

All paintings are finished with a coat of varnish to assure their protection and integrity.

USES OF OIL VARNISH ON MATTE, SATIN, AND GLOSSY SURFACES		
Matte	Satin	Glossy
• ceiling decorations • landscape panoramas	• wood elements in trompe l'oeil • people • drapes • initial panoramic layout	• marble elements in trompe l'oeil • very silky drapery • gold-leafed ornaments • mahogany and other precious woods
• on oil or acrylic	• on oil or acrylic	• on oil or acrylic
• interior use only	• interior use only	• interior and exterior use

USES OF ACRYLIC VARNISH ON MATTE, SATIN, AND GLOSSY SURFACES		
Matte	Satin	Glossy
• ceiling decorations (spread varnish with a roller because it dries very quickly) • landscape panoramas	• wood elements in trompe l'oeil • people • drapes • initial panoramic plan	• marble elements in trompe l'oeil • very silky drapery • gold-leafed ornaments • mahogany and other precious woods
• on oil or acrylic	• on oil or acrylic	• on oil or acrylic
• interior use only	• interior use only	• interior and exterior use

There are some advantages and disadvantages to oil and acrylic varnishes. Oil varnish may have a tendency to yellow; acrylic varnish won't yellow, and is completely invisible and odorless, but is never as shiny as an oil varnish.

PREPARATION OF SURFACES

Tracing Paper
No particular preparation is necessary for this surface, and it is ready for decoration. Tracing paper provides a very stable surface, and you can work in your studio.

Polyester canvas
The polyester canvas surface is of large dimension and is ready-to-use. The small pores in the fabric absorb color well and make it very durable. Another advantage to working on this surface is being able to work directly in your studio.

Walls
A careful preparation of the wall, involving several layers of lacquer, is crucial to obtain the perfect foundation.

In all cases—whether using tracing paper, canvas, or walls—the mediums used to paint the decorations remain the same: acrylic ink and oil.

REPRODUCTION TECHNIQUES / ENLARGEMENT

The traditional reproduction technique of using a grid of squares permits you to enlarge motifs to specific dimensions. For example, a one inch or one centimeter square on a model can be transcribed into ten-inch or ten-centimeter squares on the painting surface.

Transparency Projector

First, trace the sketch or model onto transparency paper. The smaller the reproduction on the transparency paper the better. Then, use the transparency projector to project the desired size of the model on whatever surface you choose (wall, canvas, etc.) Finally, carefully trace the enlarged image on the surface. This may take several hours.

Slide Projector

The use of a slide projector is very limited, but you may project a slide on the desired surface, and proceed as above.

Another traditional method for duplicating repeating motifs which is very useful is to use a perforated stencil dusted using a "pounce bag" (a small porous pocket of fabric filled with a fine pigment such as talc or yellow ochre) in order to transfer a design to a support. The stencil may be made by laying out the desired design on sturdy, slightly thick tracing paper and pricking holes along the contours of the design with a heavy needle held in a cork.

Particular emphasis should be placed on the importance of the initial step of reproduction onto your chosen surface. A well-done reproduction will simplify all the work to come and will have an important impact on the final result.

ARCHITECTURE

Page 15: Detail, A view of
Corsica, France

Right: Study of the village of
Clisson, Brittany

002

003

004

005

Opposite and above:
Details, Study of the village of Clisson

007

008

Opposite: "Between sky and earth"

Above: Detail

Left: Sketch

Opposite: "Antique Landscape"

Above: Detail

011

012

Opposite: Alcove with magpie and Olaf

Above: Detail

Gatefold:
Fountain and trellis panorama

015

Opposite: "The Lover's Temple," from a park in Versailles

Above: Detail

016

Above: "Ibis temple," in monochromatic green

Opposite: Details

017

018

019

Above and opposite: Details, "Ibis temple"

020

ARCHITECTURE *38*

022

Opposite: "Light," painted in monochromatic red

Above: Detail

023

Detail, "Light"

024

025

Top: **Artifacts of past civilizations**

Bottom: **Sketch**

027

Opposite: "Indiscretion"

Above: Detail

Study of an Italian interior

A view of Corsica, France

ARCHITECTURE   48

031

Opposite: "Clisson"

Above: Detail

ARCHITECTURE   50

033

Opposite: "Woman in red," column study in perspective

Above: Detail

035

Left: "Young people and turtledoves," oval ceiling
      panorama with balustrade, Louis XVIII style

Above: Detail

036

Statue in stone and brick niche

LANDSCAPES & SKIES

Page 55: Detail, "Landscape in Pink"

Left: Waterfall and gunnera leaves

040

041

Details, Waterfall and gunnera
leaves

042

043

044

Opposite: "Landscape in pink"

Above: Detail

045

Waterfall scene mural, created in situ at the Guégan Institute

048

Study, "The New World"

046

Above: "Native American" installation
Below: Detail, sketch for "Native American"

047

049

050

Opposite and above:
Details, "Native American"

051

"Antique Panorama"

052

053

Above and opposite: Studies of skies

054

055

Study of trees

Sketch

056

057

Sky panorama for a ceiling

Landscape study

FLORA & FAUNA

059

060

Page 83: "Boulle," precious woods with marquetry

Above: Trellis and climbing plants

061

Detail

062

Above and opposite: Details, trellis and climbing plants

063

064

Magnolia blossom

065

Agave leaves

067

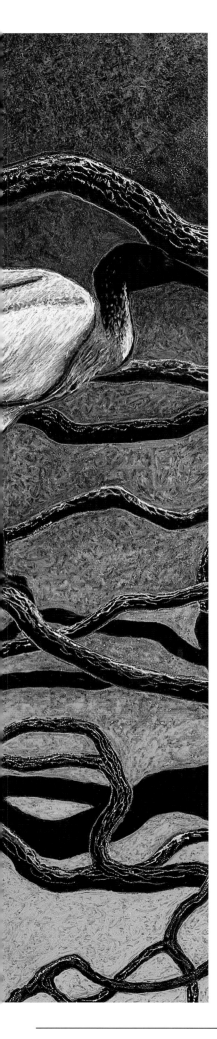

068

Gatefold: Thailand landscape

Left and above: Details

069

Detail, Thailand landscape

070

Yucca leaves

071

072

073

Top: Large plant study

Middle: Sketch

Bottom: Aucuba leaf

FLORA & FAUNA   98

075

Left: Detail, Thailand landscape,
painting on folding wood screen

Above: Sketch

Maquette Panoramique "Le Palais Oublié."

077

Opposite: "The Forgotten Palace"

Above: Detail

078

Above: Detail, "The Forgotten Palace"

Below: "The Peacock"

Opposite: Detail, Study of an Italian interior

079

081

Detail, Alcove with magpie and Olaf

082

Detail, Magpie

083

Natural jacinth

084

085

Left: Salicaire
Right: Lupine

086

Detail, "Palace of Elephants"

Detail, Study of an Italian interior

Right: Design of fig branches and leaves

Below: Study of clementines

088

089

FANTASY PANORAMAS

091

Above: Painted ceiling, "Venice"

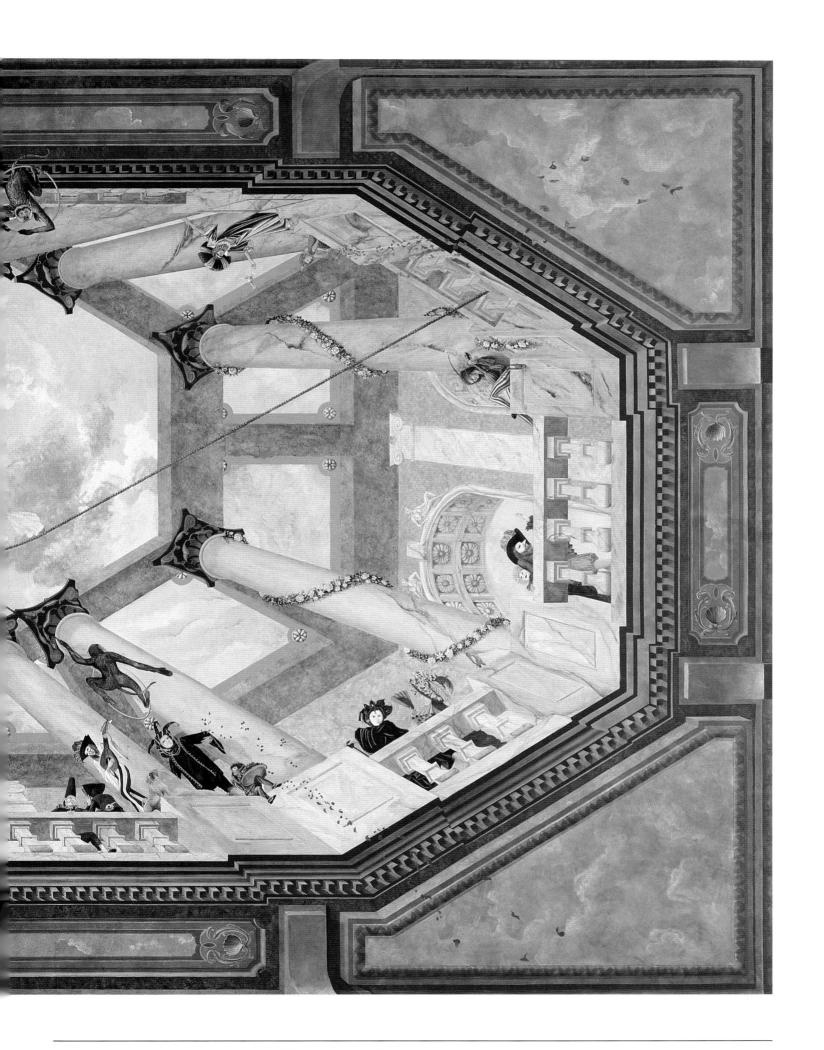

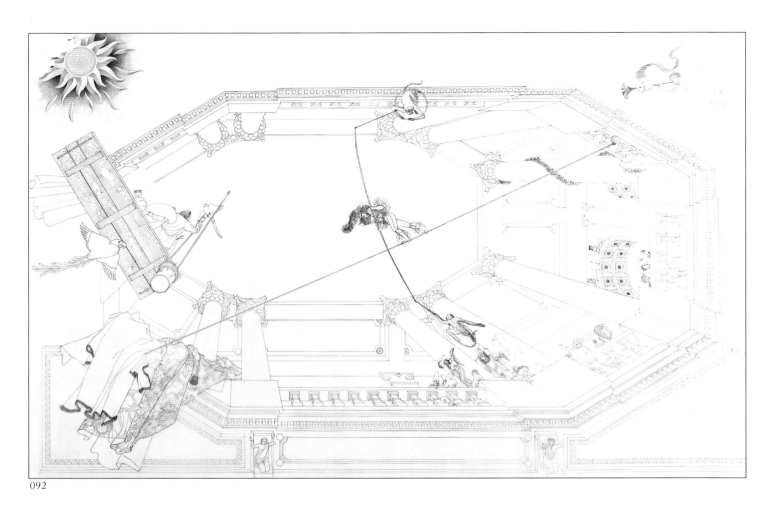

092

093

094

Opposite, top: Sketch, "Venice," in perspective

Opposite, bottom: Detail

Above: Detail

095

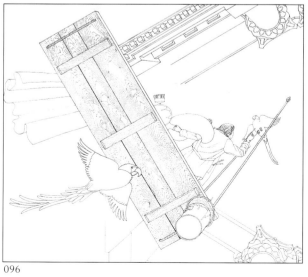

096

Above: Detail, "Venice"

Left: Detail, sketch

097

Above: Detail

Right: Detail, sketch

098

099

Above and opposite: Details, "Venice"

100

Gatefold:
"The Palace of Elephants"

102

103

Opposite and above:
Details, "The Palace of Elephants"

104

Above and opposite:
Details, "The Palace of Elephants"

105

106

Above and opposite:
Details, "The Palace of Elephants"

107

108

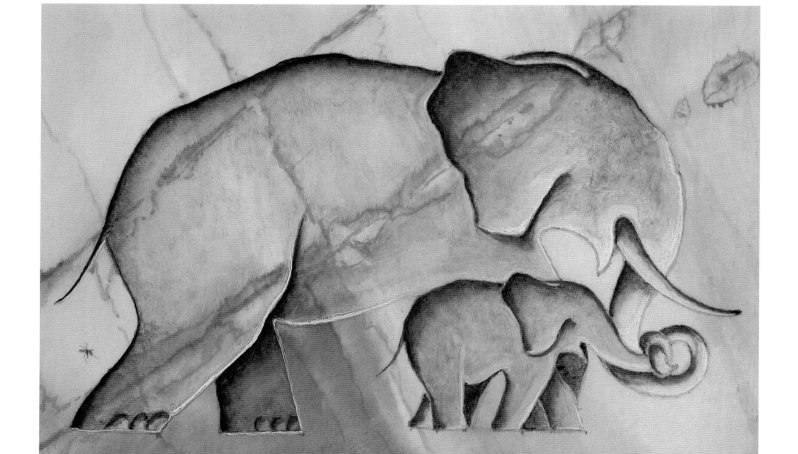

109

Details, "The Palace of Elephants"

113

Opposite and above: Details, "The Palace of Elephants"

114

Sketch, "The Palace of Elephants"

115

116

Left and above: Details, sketch, "The Palace of Elephants"

117

Detail, "The Palace of Elephants"

119

Gatefold: "Lea"

Above: Sketch, "Lea"

"Loĕa"
November 2000, Yannick Quéau

120

Above and opposite: Details, "Lea"

121

122

"Empire," interior landscape

123

Detail, "Empire"

PEOPLE & LANDSCAPES

Page 153:
Detail, "The Peacock and Lea"

"Waterlilies," ceiling
panorama painted on canvas

125

126

Above and below:
Sketches

127

"Waterlilies," full floor, ceiling
and wall panorama

128

129

Detail

130

Above and opposite: Details, "Waterlilies"

131

133

Left: "The Leopard"

Above: Detail

134

135

Opposite and above: Details, "The Leopard"

PEOPLE & LANDSCAPES 164

137

Left: "The time of childhood"

Above: Sketch

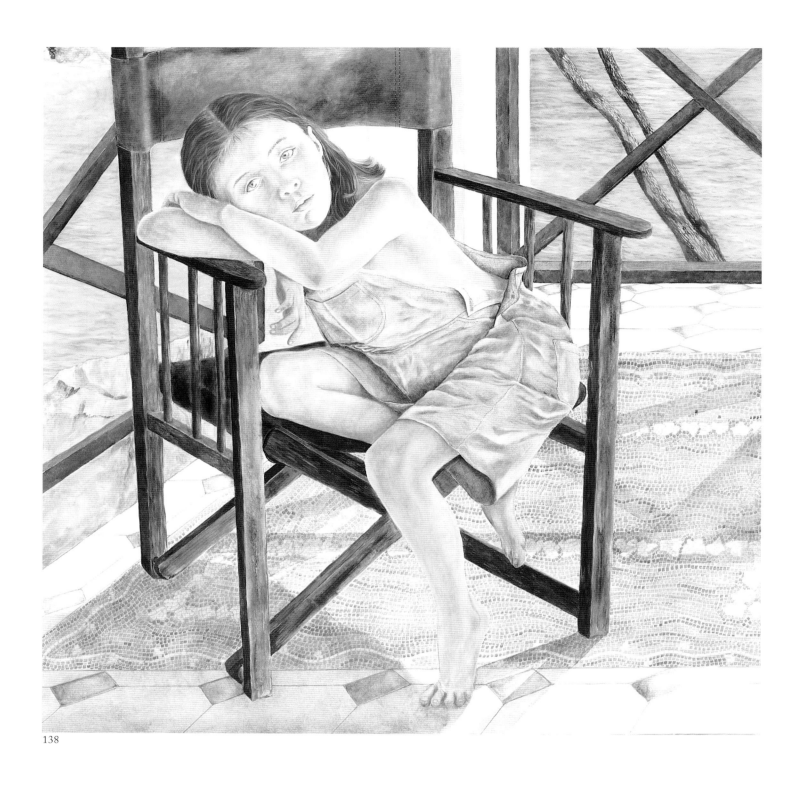

138

Above and opposite: Details, "The time of childhood"

139

140

"Alicha"

141

Above: Detail, "Alicha"

Right: Sketch

142

143

Woman among gunnerus plants

144

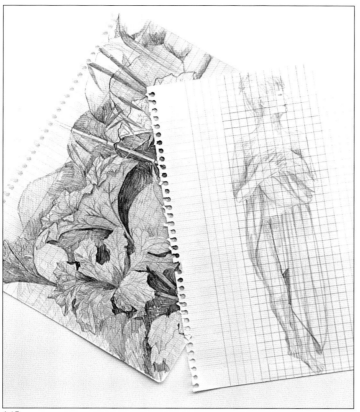

145

146

Opposite: Detail, Woman among gunnerus plants

Above: Preliminary designs

Right: Detail of preliminary design

147

Ceiling panorama, "Elephants"

148

Sketch, "Elephants"

projet pour le "Parkhaus aux Elephants" plafond. 1731 2000

149

Above and opposite: Details, "Elephants"

150

151

Above: Detail, "Elephants"

Opposite: "Woman beside pond"

152

153

"The peacock and Lea"

154

Detail, "The peacock and Lea"

WOOD & MARBLE PANELS

155

WOOD & MARBLE PANELS   186

157

Page 185: Detail, Languedoc marble panel with ornate crown

Opposite: Painted ceiling of a sky and balustrade, in perspective

Above: Cherrywood panel with galuchat incrustation and marquetry, art deco style

WOOD & MARBLE PANELS 188

159

Opposite: Languedoc marble and light oak panel

Above: Detail

160

161

Opposite: Languedoc marble panel with ornate crown, Louis XV style

Above: Detail

162

Above: Detail, Languedoc marble panel with ornate crown

Opposite: Renaissance-style table of sarrancolin and sea green marble

163

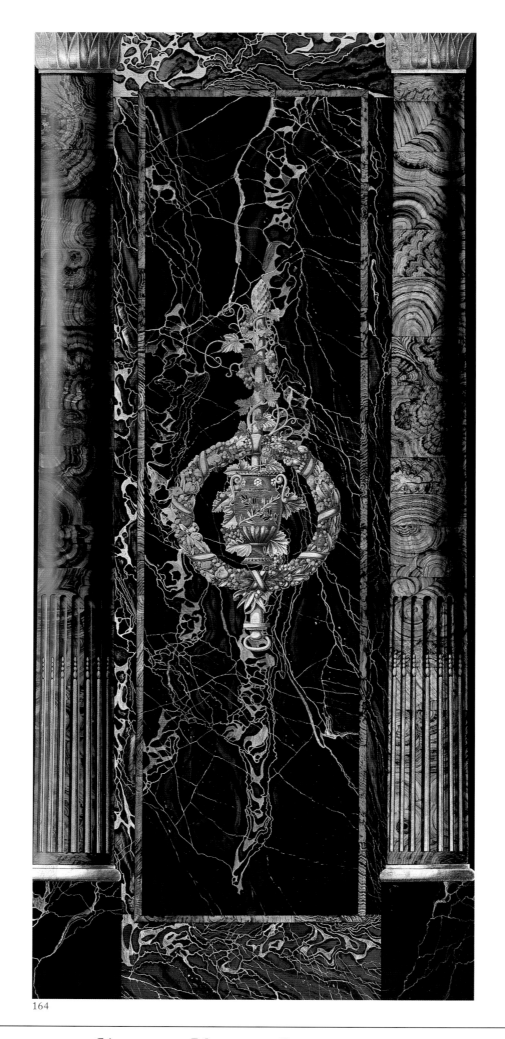

164

165

Opposite: Portor marble and malachite panel

Above: Detail

Right: Cherrywood panel with scalloped, Louis XV–style shell

Opposite: Details

166

167

168

169

170

Opposite: Renaissance-style antique marble table in sienna yellow

Above: Detail

171

Study, Renaissance-style floor from the Hôtel de Sens, Paris

Right: Sarrancolin and sea green marble panel in Louis XV style

Opposite: Details

173

174

175

176

Opposite: Monochromatic cherrywood panel with landscape and birds

Above: Detail

177

Above: Detail, Monochromatic cherrywood panel

Opposite: Walnut door panel in Louis XIII style, with drape and sash

WOOD & MARBLE PANELS   207

179

Above and opposite: Details, walnut door panel

180

181

182

Opposite: Oak panel from the Opéra Garnier, Paris

Above: Detail

Right: Oak panel with knocker

Opposite: Detail

183

WOOD & MARBLE PANELS   213

185

186

Opposite: Dark oak panel with iris tiles

Above: Detail

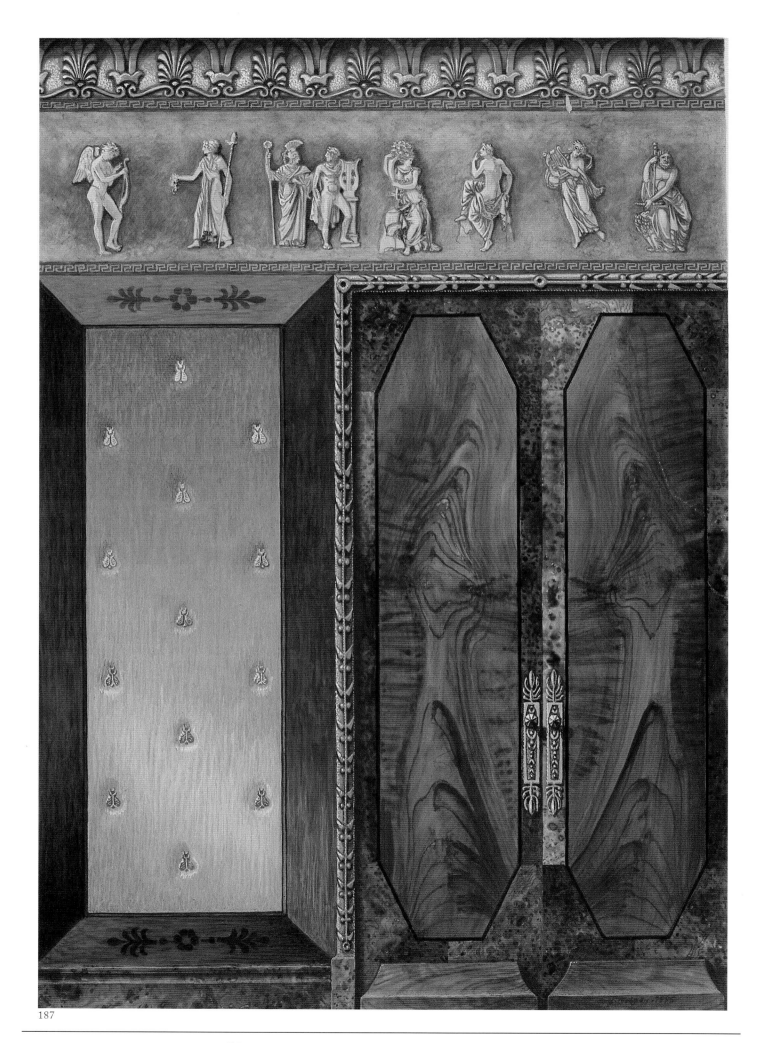

187

188

Opposite: Mahogany door with satin damask and bees, Empire style

Above: Detail

Marble panel from the
chapel floor at Versailles

189

DRAPERY

191

192

Page 219: Drapery and vase panel

Opposite: Drapery and vase on pedestal of sarrancolin marble

Above: Detail

193

194

Opposite: "Magpie and drapery"

Above: Detail

195

Above and opposite: Details, "Magpie and drapery"

196

Drapery   226

198

Opposite: Walnut panel and drapery in Louis XIII style

Above: Detail

199

Urn and lace curtains

DETAILS

Page 229: Detail, "The New World"

Right: Study of three women

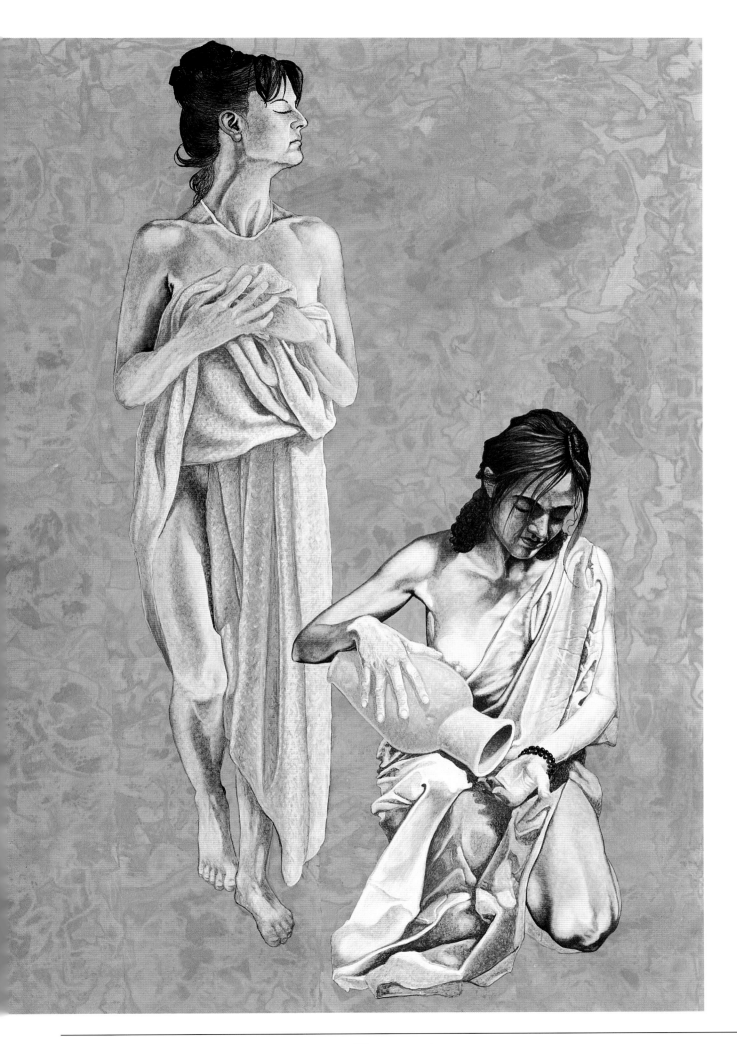

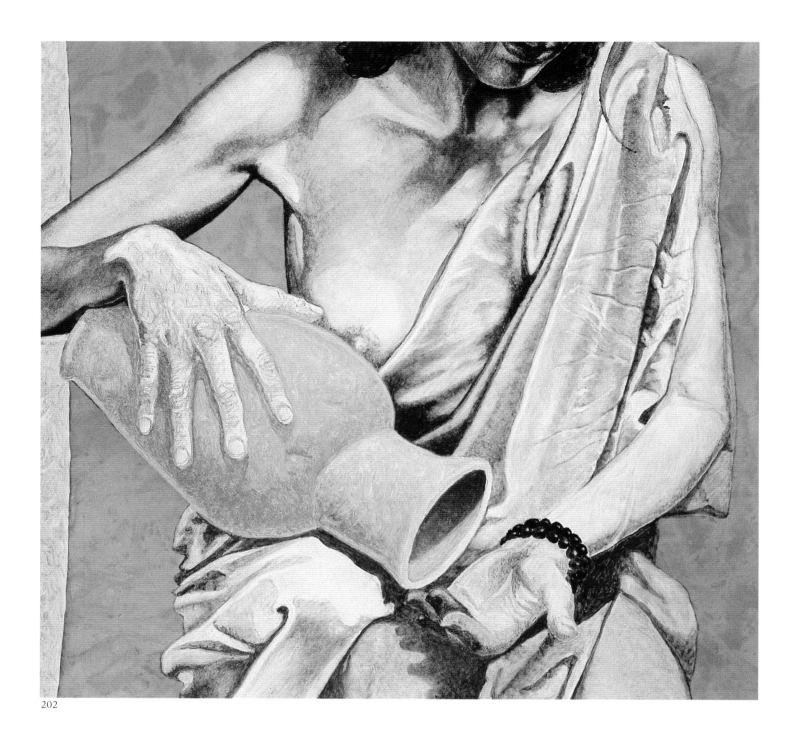

202

Detail, Study of three women

203

Study of two young girls

204

205

206

Top left:
Balustrade and
orange tree

Top right:
Vase with details
of bathers

Bottom left:
Detail, A view of
Corsica, France

Bottom right:
Gunnera leaves

207

208

Above: Study of autumn in the garden at the Guégan Institute

Below: Sketch of the waterfall scene mural created in situ at the Guégan Institute

209

Maquette Y. Guégan ad 95

210

211

Left: "Etruscan study"

Above: Detail

212

Detail, The Palace of Elephants

213

Detail, The Palace of Elephants

214

Above and opposite: Details, "Empire"

215

216

"Adrien"

217

Detail, "Adrien"

218

Detail, "The time of childhood"

INDEX

219

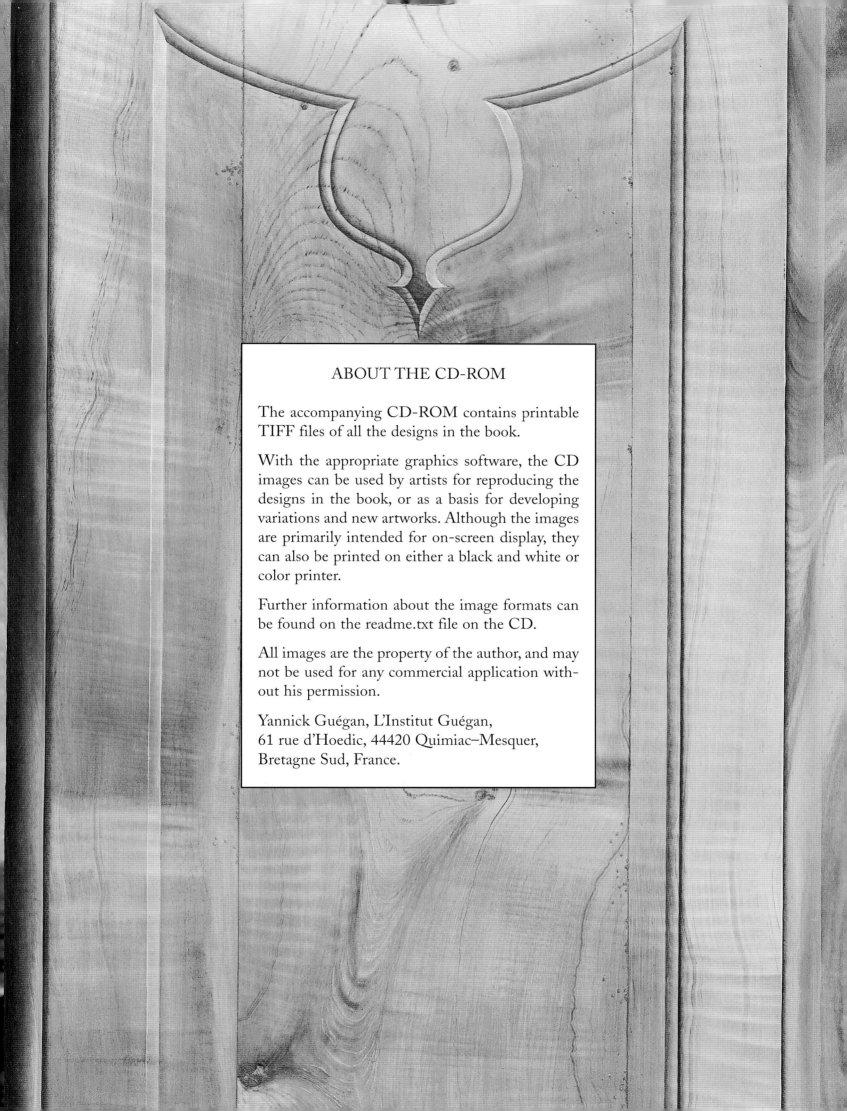

ABOUT THE CD-ROM

The accompanying CD-ROM contains printable TIFF files of all the designs in the book.

With the appropriate graphics software, the CD images can be used by artists for reproducing the designs in the book, or as a basis for developing variations and new artworks. Although the images are primarily intended for on-screen display, they can also be printed on either a black and white or color printer.

Further information about the image formats can be found on the readme.txt file on the CD.

All images are the property of the author, and may not be used for any commercial application without his permission.

Yannick Guégan, L'Institut Guégan,
61 rue d'Hoedic, 44420 Quimiac–Mesquer,
Bretagne Sud, France.